An **ama** Management Briefing

Contracts: The Move to Plain Language

Paul H. Till, Esq.
Albert F. Gargiulo

A Division of
American Management Associations

Library of Congress Cataloging in Publication Data

Till, Paul H
  Contracts, the move to plain language.

  (AMA management briefing)
  1. Contracts--United States. 2. Legal composition.
I. Gargiulo, Albert F., joint author. II. Title.
III. Series: American Management Association. AMA
management briefing.
KF801.Z9T53   346'.73'02   79-22511
ISBN 0-8144-2241-1

First Printing

Contents

	Introduction	5
1	A Brief History of Contracts	7
2	The Consumer Movement	19
3	State Law	25
4	Federal Law	32
5	Possible Future Developments	34
6	Implementation and Forms	39
7	Glossary	50

About the Authors

Paul H. Till, a member of the Bar in New Jersey and New York, is in private practice as a consultant on banking law and regulations. He is also director and general counsel of the Fortress Fund, Ltd. Mr. Till received his bachelor of arts degree from Adelphi University and his juris doctor degree from Brooklyn Law School. He is a member of the New York County Lawyers Association.

Albert F. Gargiulo is a senior program director for the finance division of the American Management Associations and a course leader for AMA classes on *Fundamentals of Finance for the Non-Financial Executive*. He is also a director of a Wall Street securities valuation and search firm and of an electronics manufacturer, and the author of *The Questioned Stock Manual*. Mr. Gargiulo holds a B.B.A. degree from Pace University and an M.B.A. in finance from St. John's University and is currently working toward a Ph.D.

Introduction

PLAIN language in contracts is a relatively new concept for business. It has already been embodied in law by New York State, and it is likely that other states will follow. Plain language in relation to contracts and agreements has a variety of other names, such as simple language, plain English, plain worded agreements, and variations and combinations on these words.

Underlying the plain language law and proposed laws is an informal movement led by writers, lawyers, consumer advocates, businessmen, educators, and others. The movement has been in existence for a number of years, although until recently it has received little publicity or attention. Many of the advocates and supporters of plain language have worked on its attainment alone and had no contact with others sharing their views, because they did not know who these others were.

Essentially, as presently embodied in law and proposed laws, the concept behind plain language is to have contracts, particularly consumer contracts, written in simple, commonly used, and widely understood words and phrases. This premise, when operational, mandates that existing highly technical legal words and phrases in contracts be replaced in rewritten contracts with plain words and that long, multipart sentences be replaced with (a series of) shorter sentences. In other words, contracts should be written in words that the average user of the document can reasonably be expected to understand. Although it's easy to state the concept, accomplishing its goal(s) is much more difficult. In the coming years business will spend many man-hours rewriting "legalese" contracts to put them into plain English. And although it's easy to state the concept, business, legal, consumer, and political circles will continue debating on how best to translate the concept into a reality. Generally the concept itself does not seem to be subject to reasonable opposition, but how it should be effectuated and executed does come under debate, and various interested groups are opposing certain proposals.

The purpose of this discussion is to introduce the plain language concept both in a general and in some specific ways. To a large degree plain language will require business to think in new terms. Right now plain language requirements apply only to consumer contracts, but in time the concept may spread to contracts between businesses and, we hope, to the laws themselves and to governmental regulations.

1

A Brief History
of Contracts

IN order to put the role of the plain language movement in proper perspective, you need a little of the history of contracts. The earliest written contracts were treaties between sovereign governments and rulers, such as those made when a princess married into the royal family of another state and a transfer of land and other property attended such a marriage; and decrees from a ruler to his people, such as those permitting hunting or berry gathering on royal lands during a certain time period.

These were not the real private contracts of which modern commerce and business is concerned, however, although they do help to provide some background. Private contracts and agreements, that is, those between two nongovernmental parties, started before writing was commonplace. A hunter, for example, would trade a deer he had killed for a certain amount of flour. This kind of early, direct, face-to-face agreement was completely executed (carried out) as soon as bargaining was completed and the terms had been agreed on. Prior to the Norman conquest of England

> there was not any law of contracts requiring the exchange or acceptance of promises to be performed in the future at all. The only ways of adding any definite security to a promise were oath and giving of pledges, which were used on solemn occasions. But business had hardly got beyond delivery against ready money between the parties both present, and there was not much room for such confidence as that on which, for example, the existence of modern banking rests.[1]

> With regard to trading disputes it seems likely that for the most part they were left to be settled by special customs of the traders, and possibly by special local tribunals in towns and markets.[1]

In theory, after the Norman conquest of England in 1066, there were two types of contracts. The first type was the sealed or formal contract. This was a written contract containing the official seals of the parties executing it on the document. To today's reader the importance of a seal or sealed document may be difficult to comprehend. It must be remembered that throughout most of the history of mankind the overwhelming majority of people were unable to read and write. Most, including even some royal rulers, were unable to write or sign their own names. In the Middle Ages the center of literacy was the clergy and its few students who were not priests. A man was identified by means of his seal, which bore his distinctive insignia or mark, often with heraldic significance.

As literacy spread the importance of the seal declined. In the past 50 years the importance of a seal on a contract has largely been reduced or abolished by statutes in Great Britain and the states of the United States; for instance, New York State passed statutes in the 1930s completely abolishing the meaning of the seal on contracts. The second type was the informal contract, which included the oral contract and the unsealed written contract.

After the Norman conquest initially there were only two varieties of contract that could be enforced in court, the sealed contract and a contract that had been completed (executed) by one party. The contract that had been completed, whether oral or written, was limited in courts to actions "for the recovery of ascertained sums of money due from a defendant for work which the

8

plaintiff had actually done, for goods which he had actually been supplied or for money he had actually lent."

Initially, unsealed written contracts that had not been carried out by one party before they were brought to court (executory unsealed contracts) could not be the basis for a suit. Gradually, by a process of crossover from other types of actions, particularly negligence, unsealed executory contracts could be the basis for a suit. Thus by the mid-1300s a suit could be brought against a boatman who had contracted to transport cattle across a river if the boatman overloaded the boat and it sank. The boatman could be sued both for breach of contract in failing to transport the cattle and for negligence.

This first expansion required a charge of misfeasance, that is, of doing something wrong. By the time of the reign of Henry VIII (1509–1547) this expansion had increased to the point where non-feasance, that is, not carrying out a contract, was a suable offense. Thus a little over 50 years later, by 1603, a party could sue in court on a sealed written contract, or an executed contract (whether oral or written), and on an executory unsealed written contract.

The doctrine of consideration as a part of contract law is unique to English-based legal systems. It is not found in ancient Roman law or in other modern European legal systems. The origins of this doctrine are obscure, but it was in effect by the late fifteenth century.

The doctrine of consideration has three separate sources. The first source was the ecclesiastical courts in England, where Roman-based canon law was expanded to include the concept that any serious promise raised a moral duty to fulfill it and therefore could be the basis of a suit. The second source was the common law courts, where an action to collect a debt was based on the fact that the defendant had received something in return for his promise of payment: work was done, money lent, or goods supplied—the so-called "quid pro quo." And the third source was the chancery (equity) courts, where great attention was paid to the real intention of the parties and inquiry was made as to the practical results of the various promises.

Actual use by the courts of the term consideration came later than the fifteenth century and not until the eighteenth century did English case law firmly establish that the presence of consideration was essential to the enforcement of an executory unsealed written contract. In 1765 it was held that consideration was the only mode of supplying evidence that the promisor intended his agreement to be binding. In Great Britain since 1778 a "promise must either be under seal or supported by consideration, whether written or unwritten"[2]

We have now traced approximately seven centuries of court-made case law on contracts. The first legislative development in contract law came toward the end of that period, and was followed by many more legislative acts. During the reign of Charles II (1660–1685) Parliament passed the original statute of frauds (29 Car II c 3). It was poorly drafted, and the rigid and conservative courts of that era were hostile to it. They rendered overly technical or capricious decisions in cases that came under the statute of frauds so as to limit its effect. Most state laws concerning fraud in the United States are derived largely from the English act, and the court decisions here have followed those of the English courts, to the effect that the statute of frauds "provides only a rule of evidence and does not affect the contract itself or its origin."[3]

The statute of frauds requires certain contracts to be in writing if the statute is to be raised as a defense. With a few variations in different states' laws, the types of contracts required to be in writing under the statute of frauds generally are:

1. A promise to answer for the debt or default of another person (guaranty and suretyship contracts).
2. Contracts for the sale of real estate or an interest in real estate.
3. Contracts for the lease of real property for more than one year.
4. Contracts for the sale of goods of more than a specific value, such as $500, depending on local state law.
5. Contracts not to be performed within one year or within a lifetime.
6. Contracts to bequeath property (leave property by will).
7. Contracts to establish a trust.
8. Conveyances or assignments of a trust in personal property or contracts to make such a transfer.
9. Promises to pay debts discharged in bankruptcy proceedings in the United States courts.
10. Contracts made in consideration of marriage.[4]

Along with the parol evidence rule, discussed below, the statute of frauds incorporates the principal premise underlying business and consumer contracts in the United States. The reasons for passing the original statute and all its successors have essentially remained the same through the years. Although the law is called the statute of frauds, the title of the original act included a descriptive phrase that noted the act was designed to prevent fraud.

The contracts embraced by the statute are of such a nature and importance that putting the agreement of the parties in writing makes its terms permanent. One can easily imagine the problems that would come up if the guarantor of a loan did not put his commitment in writing. If the borrower defaulted, the guarantor could claim that he had never been party to such an agreement. Also lenders, after a default, could claim that some other person had agreed to guarantee the loan.

Similarly, with a contract for the purchase of a house or a new car, a failure to have the agreement in writing could lead to endless wrangles between the parties concerning such details as the date of delivery or the extras and options to be included in the purchase of the main object. If apartment leases were not in writing landlords and tenants could spend all their time disputing who was responsible for heating the premises, fixing the plumbing, or repairing appliances. (As it is, with written leases, disagreements between landlords and tenants abound.)

Although a contract in writing satisfies the requirements of basic contract law of offer and acceptance, it does not necessarily eliminate other defenses. The fact that a contract is in writing does not remove the obvious requirement that the objects of the contract be legal. Also, the party against whom enforcement of the contract is sought must have received consideration in exchange for his obligations (promises) under the agreement.

The other principle underlying modern written contracts is the parol evidence rule, which developed over the years through case law and is embodied in the statute law of some jurisdictions. Subject to certain technical legal exceptions, such as fraud, which are not relevant here, this rule states that when the parties have reduced their agreement into written form, evidence cannot be offered in court of any prior or contemporaneous oral agreement that would contradict, vary, add to, or subtract from the terms embodied in the writing between the parties.[5]

The "rule is premised on the assumed intention of the parties, evidenced by their apparently complete written contract, to place their transaction beyond the uncertainties of (later) oral testimony, and the law is not inclined to defeat this presumed intention. The rule acts as a guard against fraud and perjury, infirmity of memory and the death of witnesses."[5] Without this rule, if a lender sued the co-signer of a note, the co-signer could claim that there was an oral agreement between himself and the lender that the lender would not sue him unless the prime debtor was dead. Or the purchaser of a house might claim that the seller was to paint the entire house inside and outside before the purchaser had to take title and pay for the house. A seller of merchandise might claim during a period of currency inflation that he was to be paid in gold at its value on the date of execution of the contract months before.

Subject to the conditions put on contracts, mainly by statutory enactments discussed later, the statute of frauds and the parol evidence rule provide business with the certainty necessary to operate in the modern commercial environment. Although nothing can prevent the occurrence of default, these two legal premises allow one to know what he is contracting to do and what he will receive in return. Beyond the few examples given above, it is left to the reader to imagine the chaotic conditions that would exist without fixed written contracts.

The earliest development in contract law in the United States was in the federal Constitution. Article I, Section 10, Paragraph 1 provides that "No State shall . . . pass . . . law impairing the obligation of contracts. . . ." This constitutional provision was written at the behest of the propertied class of the 1780's, who feared that state legislatures, responding to popular political desires, might pass laws under which debtors and tenants would be allowed out of their obligations. This provision prohibits the states from altering by law any "existing" contracts; it does not bar a state from passing laws that would affect and control the terms of future contracts.

Interestingly, the terms of this constitutional provision do not apply to Congress. At the time, the drafters of the Constitution did not envision that the federal government, even with its exclusive power over interstate commerce, could ever be involved in matters of daily commerce under the federal system. However, even though through the years the federal government has become increasingly involved in commercial matters, Congress has not passed laws that would retroactively affect existing contracts, except in the 13th Amendment.

The 13th Amendment to the U.S. Constitution was adopted in 1865 as a result of the Civil War. It provides that "Neither slavery nor involuntary servitude, except as a punishment for crime whereof the party shall have been duly convicted, shall exist within the United States. . . ." This so-called "Abolition Amendment" affected existing contracts in that slaves had been purchased by their owners under contracts legal at the time of purchase and involuntary servitude was at times a matter of contract between a party such as a farmer or mill owner and the parent of a child sent to work for that party.

From this point in time the major developments in the law of written contracts have come mainly from Congress, legislatures, and regulatory agencies—not the courts. These developments have been mostly to prohibit certain terms, require certain terms, and require certain wording in contracts. Thus by and large the changes have meant restricting and limiting the total freedom to contract. Three areas of federal legislation had a great effect on the right to contract.

The Interstate Commerce Act was passed by Congress in 1887. It originally applied only to railroads. It created the Interstate Commerce Commission to see that rates were reasonable and otherwise to regulate railroads and it prohibited contract terms that resulted in unfair charges such as discriminatory rates, drawbacks, and rebates. These contractual terms had been used by the railroads and major shippers and customers to the detriment of small shippers. After court decisions hampered the powers of the commission, laws in 1903, 1910, 1913, and 1935 reestablished these powers, expanded them, and gave the commission jurisdiction over telephone and telegraph companies, trucking operations, and bus carriers.

Beginning about 1880 monopolies began to sprout up in many important and basic industries. The movement to restrict such monopolies resulted in Congress passing the Sherman Anti-Trust Act in 1890. The Act directly banned certain contracts. It stated, in part, "Every contract, or conspiracy, in restraint of trade or commerce among the several states, or with foreign nations, is hereby declared to be illegal." This policy was expanded and modified by the Clayton Antitrust Act in 1914. The Clayton Act removed labor and agricultural organizations from coverage and control by antitrust laws. With regard to contracts it prohibited price discrimination that encouraged monopolies and agreements on the part of the purchaser not to buy from the seller's competitors (typing contracts).

In 1914 Congress passed the Federal Trade Commission Act, which was designed to prevent unfair methods of competition in interstate commerce. The commission created by the act had as its initial goals the elimination of mislabeling and adulteration of products, untrue patent claims, and two contract-related matters: trade boycotts and arrangements for the maintenance of resale prices. The powers of the commission have grown through the years, until today it is a major factor in business, consumer affairs, and contracts.

It was not until after World War I and more particularly after World War II that the written consumer contract developed. Up until this time most written contracts were strictly for business purposes, such as the purchase of a farm or business, the purchase of stocks of goods or commodities, the formation of a partnership or corporation, the issuance of stocks or other securities, and the building of structures. The only exceptions were insurance policies and agreements for the purchase of residential real estate. For example, until after World War I personal consumer loans did not exist.

The expanding economy and increase in standard of living by a major portion of the population of the United States after World War I led to a wider area of consumer purchases. Such consumer purchases and concomitant borrowings led to the creation of specialized contracts and agreements—consumer contracts. Among the consumer agreements that have come into existence since World War I or have developed significantly from simpler earlier forms are:

- Home improvement construction contracts, such as for aluminum siding or insulation.
- Securities and commodities brokerage margin account contracts.
- Cemetery plot purchase contracts.
- Retail goods layaway plan purchase contracts.

- Mail order retail goods purchase plan agreements, such as a record or book club or the Franklin Mint.
- Educational/vocational training contracts, such as for radio/television repair or computer programming.
- Motor vehicle purchase contracts and warranty-service agreements.
- Bank overdraft checking account credit agreements.
- Bank and finance company unsecured personal loan notes and secured personal loan notes and security agreements, such as for home improvements or automobile purchases.
- Bank credit card agreements, such as Master Charge and VISA.
- Private credit card contracts, such as American Express and Diner's Club.
- Retail store credit card or credit account contracts for such stores as Sears Roebuck.
- Automobile liability and comprehensive insurance policies.
- Homeowners' and tenants' liability and comprehensive insurance policies.
- Medical/surgical health insurance plans, both individual and group, such as Blue Cross/Blue Shield.
- Appliance warranties.
- Moving and storage agreements.
- Automobile, truck, and trailer rental contracts, including renting a car for the weekend and lease purchase contracts.
- Travel club plan contracts.
- Small investment franchising agreements, such as between Avon Products Inc. and their independent sales personnel.
- Apartment leases.
- Condominium real estate purchase contracts.
- Cooperative apartment purchase contracts and membership agreements.

As can be seen from this list, the range of contracts in the consumer field is quite wide and affects almost every area of the private sector of the American economy. Because of its range and impact and various abuses or so-called abuses, various laws and governmental regulations have been formulated and passed through the years, largely at the behest of reform and consumer groups. These establish certain terms and provisions in contracts and prohibit or limit others. Additionally, court decisions have placed certain limitations on business with regard to consumer agreements.

Although the insurance industry is one of the very few major interstate businesses that is not controlled or regulated in a major way by the federal government there is a great deal of regulation by individual states. The actual wording of insurance policy clauses or their content is established by statutes or set by insurance regulatory agencies in most states.

Residential leases, particularly in urban states, are subject to a variety of laws and governmental regulations. In some states the landlord must pay interest to the tenant on the amount of the rent security deposit he holds under the terms of the lease. There are legal limitations on the grounds for which a tenant can be evicted from a residence for a breach of the lease. There are also limitations on the methods and procedures by which the eviction is carried out. In a somewhat related area, requirements and restrictions have been placed on the contractual terms in agreements by which condominium and cooperative real estate is sold.

By a regulation commonly known as the (anti) holder in due course rule established by the U.S. Federal Trade Commission and adopted by the federal bank regulatory agencies—the Federal Reserve Board and U.S. Comptroller of the Currency—an ancient common law contract legal principle was abolished in the 1970's. The old law stated that when a note (negotiable instrument) was transferred by one owner/holder to another, the debtor or maker could not raise defenses against the new owner on the note if the note itself did not contain notice of such a defense.

This common law holder in due course doctrine was intended to expedite commerce and make the transfer of commercial paper more certain. Under the doctrine a seller of goods who was paid with a note could sell that note to his bank, and the buyer could not refuse to pay the note even if the goods turned out to be defective or less than agreed upon with the seller.

After investigation the Federal Trade Commission abolished the rule, because it was found that it was being used in an abusive manner by sellers and because it was believed that banks and other buyers of such notes had more economic power to control the sellers from whom they bought such notes; that is, banks would refuse to buy notes from sellers against whom there were a great number of complaints. (This Federal Trade Commission rule does not apply to normal checks or nonconsumer notes, to which the common law still applies.)

The U.S. Truth in Lending Act and its subordinate Federal Reserve Regulation Z require that lenders to personal loan borrowers disclose in detail in writing all the costs of credit. These disclosures are a part of the total loan agreement, and a failure by the lender to comply can create a defense for the borrower. Unfortunately, the Regulation Z required disclosures have become so detailed and complex that many borrowers do not understand them. This has led to a congressional movement to simplify Truth in Lending.

The U.S. Equal Credit Opportunity Act and Regulation B formulated under it by the Federal Reserve Bank both set restrictions. A creditor cannot deny credit on such civil rights grounds as race, creed, national origin, sex, age, or marital status; and limits are set on a creditor's contractual ability to require a borrower to have his spouse cosign the note. These are obvious and, most people would agree, proper restrictions on the freedom to contract.

A number of state laws and court rules limit late charges and attorneys' fees provisions for default in contracts and notes. For instance, in New York an attorney who is an employee of a bank cannot collect any attorneys' fees for collection of defaulted personal notes. The percentage or amount that can be charged as late (payment) fees is frequently set by state law.

Consumer product warranties are controlled and subject to the U.S. Moss-Magnuson Act. Government restrictions exist on the amount of consumer credit that a bank or finance company may extend to an individual borrower and the percentage of credit that can be allowed to an individual for the margin purchase of stocks and other securities. In recent years an increasing number of states have been placing or looking into placing legal restrictions on the sellers of franchises to individual buyers.

Some licensing laws prohibit or restrict the right of business to make or enforce a contract unless that business or businessman is officially licensed by the government. Aside from the obvious professions such as medicine and law this extends to real estate broker/salesmen, building contractors and plumbers, and insurance agents. Although there are charges that such licensing laws are designed to create or protect a trade monopoly in some areas, their real purpose is protection of the consumer, which is frequently accomplished through the contract area of the law.

To a certain extent state usury–interest rate limitation laws on personal loans are a consumer contract measure. However, although many of these laws have been revised since World War II, their origin dates back to ancient times. Their background is wider than the basis of Anglo-American law. Usury laws come from an earlier European culture—from Christian Biblical doctrine prohibiting overcharging for the borrowing or use of money, prohibiting traditional usury, and condemning the usurer.

A recent legal restriction for the protection of the consumer on the freedom to contract has been the so-called "cooling off" period. For example, when a buyer or borrower (other than for a first mortgage) is going to pledge his or her residential real estate as security for the contract or note, he or she must be given a certain time period, such as three days, after the agreement is signed before it becomes effective and the second mortgage on the home can be recorded. During this cooling-off period the consumer may cancel the contract or loan without any penalty. Such cooling-off period requirements were established to counter the effect of sharp sales practices, in part in the home improvement construction industry.

The above is a broad, sweeping overview of changes made to contract law, mainly in recent years, concerning consumer contracts. It is by no means exhaustive, and many other laws and regulations could be included. Although some of the standards and restrictions imposed on consumer contracts by law arose from good government and general reform movements, most of those enacted in recent years have been the result of the political efforts mounted by the so-called consumer movement.

---

[1]Frederic W. Maitland and Francis C. Montague, *A Sketch of English Legal History* (G. P. Putnam's Sons, New York, 1915).

[2]The above history, from the time of the Norman conquest, is based on Edgar Hammond, *A Concise Legal History* (Sweet and Maxwell Ltd, London, 1921).

[3]Clarence D. Ashley, *The Law of Contracts* (Brown and Company, Boston, 1911).

[4]William J. Casey, *Lawyer's Desk Book* (new revised second edition) (Institute for Business Planning Inc., New York, 1971).

[5]Jerome Prince, *Richardson on Evidence* (ninth edition) (Brooklyn Law School, Brooklyn, N.Y., 1964).

2

The Consumer
Movement

THE consumer movement has had a sizable impact on many of the laws enacted by the state and federal governments and on the actions taken and rules enacted by many of the independent regulatory agencies in recent years. Ralph Nader and Nader's Raiders have been perhaps the most prominent private group in the consumer field for the past few years but it is important to note that consumer protection groups have been present on the American scene for some time.

Product safety councils include members of the general public or are consumer based. Also, the Better Business Bureau has provided noteworthy service to the public it was organized to champion for many years. The existence of such private consumer protection groups has led to the creation of governmental consumer protection agencies or consumer advocates in some parts of the country. As noted above, the passage of many of the laws affecting the substance of consumer contracts for the protection of the general public are in part a result of work by such groups.

The consumer movement has grown through the years because of a number of economic and societal factors. Just as the expansion of business and industry into large corporations in part led to the growth of labor unions to represent the workers in a less violent way, it also led to the growth of consumer groups. Such groups were increasingly necessary to deal with large business organizations about many of the problems that arose in daily commerce.

In many instances it would be impossible for a business to deal with each consumer effectively. Sometimes government agencies created to handle problems that arise in the consumer sector of the economy became so tied up in bureaucracy and red tape that it was necessary for a private outside consumer group to come into existence to spur the agency into action; public utility commissions are an example. In some cases, a consumer group could more easily take a broad view of problems over a broad field and deal with them than a government agency limited to one field, such as transportation, or a well-meaning businessman basically confined to his one industry, could. It has also been the American experience that people who share some common interest tend to form, join, or in some way support groups that express their point of view or feelings in that domain.

The expansion of the American economy and population since World War I has brought many more people into the market for consumer goods beyond the bare necessities of food and clothes. Outlined in Section 1 are contracts covering some of the many consumer goods and services that have become available to Americans in this time period. Along with these products certain difficulties and problems evolved. Some of the problems could be dealt with by existing governmental institutions. Others initially could not be handled by the public authorities, causing consumer activist groups to come into being and to grow.

Through the years corresponding with the post-Civil War industrial expansion in the United States, the contracts used in business became longer, more detailed, and more complex in their wording. With the evolution and growth of consumer purchases and consumer contracts, the same factor of increased complexity has become a part of the development of these contracts.

A consumer loan installment note in use about 1950, prior to various court decisions and statutory changes, was often a legal-sized document with small type; it was wordy, full of complicated legalese, and had a confusing design with many blanks that needed to be filled in. By the mid-1970s a personal installment loan note read as shown in Exhibit 1. An example of a so-called plain language personal loan installment note is shown in Exhibit 2.

Several factors contributed to the creation of a complex consumer contract.

1. All, not just consumer, contracts became more complex. This in turn is attributable in part to the growth of a more complicated American way of life, the replacement of a rural society with an urban/suburban civilization, and the increased transience of the population after World War II.

2. Advances in printing allowed a great deal more small print to be placed on a page or on both sides of a page. This advance provided contract writers with more space on which to write long and complicated contractual terms.

3. Some commercial enterprises deliberately lengthened their consumer contracts and made the wording complex and obtuse. They did this to discourage consumers from reading agreements before signing them or questioning what they read.

4. The legal profession made agreements more complex. Through the years, with attorneys writing, revising, and rewriting consumer contracts, the wording and phraseology became increasingly more specialized into the terminology of the law.

5. Court decisions in different jurisdictions through the years abetted the growing complexity. Where such decisions were adverse to or had adverse implications for business, the response of business was, wherever possible, to revise agreements. Such revisions were made in order to eliminate, limit, or circumvent the effects of an adverse court ruling. A number of such revisions would add not only to the length of the document, but also to the amount of legal verbiage it contained.

6. New requirements imposed and mandated by statutes or governmental regulations led to modifications to consumer contracts, which generally made them more complicated. Statutorily required provisions in tenants' leases have had this effect. The Truth in Lending disclosure requirements lengthened personal loan notes and added to their complexity. The provisions of insurance policies dictated by statute or drafted by or approved by state insurance authorities are generally quite lengthy, verbose, and complicated.

Exhibit 1. Shortened installment loan form of the mid-1970s.

DEPARTMENT   NOTE

$............   ...., ..., 19.........

FOR VALUE RECEIVED, I (we jointly and severally) promise to pay to the order of

THE   NATIONAL BANK (hereinafter called the "Bank")

the sum of ....   Dollars ($.......................)

at any office of the Bank, in .... consecutive monthly payments of which the first
.... payments shall be $.............. each and the last payment shall be
$................ The first payment shall be made on ...., 19 ...., and subsequent
payments shall be made on the same day of each month thereafter until this note has been paid in full.

Whenever any payment hereunder is delayed ten (10) days beyond the due date therefor, I (we jointly and
severally) promise to pay to the holder hereof on or before the next payment date liquidated damages of five cents
($.05) for each dollar of such delayed payment.

If any payment is not made hereunder when due, the entire sum owing hereunder shall at the option of the
holder hereof become immediately due and payable.

Each party hereto, whether as maker, indorser or otherwise, hereby (1) waives all demand for payment,
presentment for payment, notice of dishonor, protest and notice of protest and any and all extensions of time for
the payment of all of any part of the indebtedness evidenced hereby (whether by means of a renewal note or notes
or otherwise), (2) authorizes the holder hereof to cause the signature of one or more makers or indorsers to be
added hereto at any time or from time to time, (3) agrees that the holder hereof may at any time or from time to
time debit all or any part of the sum owing hereunder to any deposit or account now or hereafter maintained by
him with the holder hereof, even though this note be unmatured, without notice, and without thereby affecting
his liability hereunder for any part of the indebtedness evidenced hereby which is not so debited or applied, and
(4) if this Note is not paid at maturity or upon default, agrees that all expenses of collection hereof, including
reasonable attorneys' fees, may be added to the sum due hereunder, to be paid as a part thereof. Any unpaid
balance may be paid at any time and that portion of the Finance Charge in excess of $15 shall be refunded based
on the "Rule of 78's".

SIGNATURES   ADDRESSES
(write in full)   (give complete address)

(1) Borrower ....   (L.S.) ....

(2) Co-Maker ....   (L.S.) ....
              (Wife or Husband of Borrower)

              (DIRECT LOANS)   **ORIGINAL**

Exhibit 2. Simplified loan form in plain language and relatively large type.

1. BORROWER'S PROMISE TO PAY

In return for a loan that I have received, I promise to pay .... Dollars (this amount will be called "principal"), ... plus interest, to the order of the Lender. The Lender is .... I understand that the Lender may transfer this Note. The Lender or anyone who takes this Note by transfer and who is entitled to receive payments under this Note will be called the "Note holder."

2. INTEREST

I will pay interest at a rate of .... percent per year. Interest will be charged on that part of principal which has not been paid. Interest will be charged beginning on the date of this Note and continuing until the full amount of principal has been paid.

3. PAYMENTS

I will pay principal and interest by making payments every month. Each of my monthly payments will be in the amount of .... Dollars (US $ ....).

I will make my monthly payments on the .... day of each month beginning on .... , 19......... . I will make these payments every month until I have paid all of the principal and interest and any other charges, described below, that I may owe under this Note. If, on .... , I still owe amounts under this Note, I will pay all those amounts, in full, on that date.

I will make my monthly payments at .... , or at a different place if required by the Note holder.

23

The widespread existence of complicated consumer contracts of many types for the past 20 years led to a number of efforts to simplify agreements. It is doubtful that any one person or group can claim to be the leader of the plain language movement. Both within and outside the legal profession people have acknowledged that agreements had become far too technical, complicated, and confusing.

The first large-scale public step in the direction of less complicated and more understandable consumer contracts occurred with consumer installment loan notes at Citibank (First National City Bank) in New York City. These notes were created for Citibank under a program headed by Allen Siegel. The purpose of the program was to simplify the wording and eliminate the technical legalese in the notes. In addition, there was a separate advertising and marketing aspect. Citibank was able to promote its consumer loans partly on the basis of the simplicity and clarity of the terms in its new notes. Some other banks followed Citibank's lead in the years that followed.

However, beyond the creation of the Citibank consumer notes, other factors led to the spread of the simple or plain language movement. Numerous consumer groups and part of the public interest segment of the legal profession had for some time been making requests and demands that consumer agreements be written in everyday language. Also, the average reading comprehension levels of eighth-grade students and high school graduates is on the decline.

With these different elements at work at the same time as a shift in the broad philosophical attitude of the American public toward getting "back to basics," such as the drives to protect the natural environment and to reduce government activities, the idea of simplified wording in contracts—the plain language movement, as it is often called—soon came to the attention of elected representatives and other government officials.

3

State Law

THE first state that took legislative action on plain language was New York. A law was introduced and passed in 1977 with very little input by business interests, either because they believed that the bill would never pass and/or because there was no objection to the substantive concept underlying it. However, without such input from business interests, the original version of the law had some aspects that could have made compliance unreasonably difficult. Consequently, partially successful efforts were made to amend the law. Although the amended law is still vague in certain respects and has some other drawbacks, it is an improvement over the original act. This law, which became effective on Nov. 1, 1978, is part of the New York General Obligations Law, and reads as follows:

Section 5-702. Requirements for Use of Plain Language in Consumer Agreements.

a. Every written agreement entered into after November 1, 1978, for the lease of space to be occupied for residential purposes, or to which a consumer is a party and the money, property or service which is the subject of the transaction is primarily for personal, family or household purposes must be:

1. Written in a clear and coherent manner using words with common and every day meanings;
2. Appropriately divided and captioned by its various sections.

Any creditor, seller or lessor who fails to comply with this subdivision shall be liable to a consumer who is a party to a written agreement governed by this subdivision in an amount equal to any actual damages sustained plus a penalty of fifty dollars. The total class action penalty against any such creditor, seller or lessor shall not exceed ten thousand dollars in any class action or series of class actions arising out of the use by a creditor, seller or lessor of an agreement which fails to comply with this subdivision. No action under this subdivision may be brought after both parties to the agreement have fully performed their obligation under such agreement, nor shall any creditor, seller or lessor who attempts in good faith to comply with this subdivision be liable for such penalties. This subdivision shall not apply to agreements involving amounts in excess of fifty thousand dollars nor prohibit the use of words or phrases or forms of agreement required by state or federal law, rule or regulation or by a governmental instrumentality.

b. A violation of the provisions of subdivision a. of this section shall not render any such agreement void or voidable nor shall it constitute:

1. A defense to any action or proceeding to enforce such agreement; or
2. A defense to any action or proceeding for breach of such agreement.

c. In addition to the above, whenever the attorney general finds that there has been a violation of this section, he may proceed as provided in subdivision 12. of section 63 of the executive law.

As of this writing New Jersey appears to be the next state that will enact a plain (English) language law. The New Jersey assembly adopted the following bill on June 22, 1978.

1. Title. This act shall be known and may be cited as the "Plain Language Agreement Act."
2. Understandable terms required. Written agreements

covered under this act shall only permit the following terms:

a. Terms whose meaning is generally understandable to persons other than persons with more than a twelfth grade reading level, professionals or specialists in the particular field. These terms shall be excluded when their generally understood meaning is contradictory to the applicable legal or technical meaning.

b. Necessary technical specifications of a product or service.

3. Clear composition required. Language and structure used shall meet the following requirements:

a. Sections shall be appropriately divided and captioned.

b. All text shall be no less than 10 point type.

c. Sentences shall not have unnecessary length or degree of complexity.

d. Cross references that are unnecessarily confusing shall not be used.

e. Definitions which are contradictory to generally understood meanings shall not be used.

f. Sentences that have double negatives or exceptions to exceptions shall not be used.

g. Sentences and sections shall not be arranged in a confusing sequence. They shall be in a logical order.

4. Written agreements covered. This act shall only apply to standard form agreements in which the subject of the transaction is primarily for personal, family or household purposes. It is limited to the following transactions:

a. A real estate transaction.

b. A transaction involving rental of a residential unit within premises which include more than three rental units.

c. A transaction for money, personal property, a product or service, including insurance, involving less than $50,000.00.

5. Language covered. This act shall not apply to the following language:

a. Language which is expressly defined, required or permitted by Federal or State law or regulation.

b. Language which is drafted as a result of bona fide negotiations between the parties to the agreement, or for sole use in one agreement.

6. Persons excluded. This act shall not apply to any of the following persons:

a. A creditor, seller or lessor using the agreement in businesses producing less than $100,000.00 gross annually or in nonbusiness uses.

b. A borrower, purchaser or lessee who is represented by an attorney. This fact shall be established by the attorney's signed statement on the agreement.

7. Violators' liability. Any creditor, seller or lessor who violates this act shall be liable to a borrower, purchaser or lessee who is a party to the agreement. The liability shall be determined by a court of competent jurisdiction to be equal to the sum of the following:

a. Actual damages sustained.

b. Punitive damages not over $500.00.

c. Costs of the action.

d. Reasonable attorneys' fees.

Rights and remedies under any other law shall continue.

8. Class action limitation. The total class action punitive damages against any person shall not exceed $50,000.00. This includes a series of class actions arising out of the use of identical standard form agreements.

9. Enforcement constraint. No punitive damages under this act shall be enforced against any person who attempts in good faith to comply with this act. No punitive damages shall be enforced where the text of an agreement achieves a minimum Flesch scale readability score of fifty. The Flesch scale readability score shall be determined by the Flesch readability formula. The formula is set forth in The Act of Readable Writing by Rudolf Flesch. Also no punitive damages shall be awarded after all parties to the agreement have fully performed their obligations under the agreement.

10. Agreement remains in force. A violation of this act shall not render any agreement void or voidable. A violation of this act shall not constitute a defense to any other action or proceeding for enforcement or breach of agreement. No provision for renewal of an agreement shall be invalid merely because compliance with this act changes the form of the renewed agreement.

11. Waiver prohibited. No agreement shall contain a waiver of any rights under this act.

12. Processing fee authorized. Where any State agency required by law to process agreements finds this act will cause it additional expense, it may charge an appropriate fee. The fee shall only be charged applicants for a total of 2 years. It shall not exceed the amount needed to recover actual expenses.

13. Enactment. This act shall take effect on the three hundred and sixty-fifth day after the date of enactment, except that section 12, and steps necessary for its implementation, shall take effect immediately.

As of this writing the New Jersey senate has revised the plain language act and sent the new version to the assembly for passage. By the time you read this a law may have already been passed. The concept underlying the plain language movement did not appear to have any opposition in New Jersey, although there may be some requests for changes so that the law is reasonable, practical, workable, and not unduly costly to comply with. In the meantime, New Jersey did pass a Life and Health Insurance Policy Language Simplification Act on Aug. 6, 1979. Similar goals can be expected elsewhere.

Numerous other state legislatures are considering passage of plain language laws of similar or differing formats. Among the other states known to the authors to have proposed plain language bills before their legislatures are Connecticut, Hawaii, Indiana, Massachusetts, Michigan, and Pennsylvania. Reportedly such bills are also before the legislatures of approximately a dozen other states. The adoption of a plain language law by one of the nation's leading commercial states—New York—will certainly encourage passage of similar laws in many other states in the next few years. And therein lies a problem for businessmen and other interests.

Different states will enact similar, but not identical, laws. As can be seen by a reading of the New York law and the bill passed by the New Jersey assembly, there are differences concerning the types of consumer contracts covered or to be covered. The proposed New Jersey law would cover insurance policies but the enacted New York law does not seem to encompass insurance agreements. If the number of state plain language laws were to increase to five types, difficulties and confusion could arise, particularly for interstate businesses.

For instance, if a major retailer who is located in (state) ABC, which does not have a plain language law or has one type of plain language law, sells goods under a written contract and/or credit agreement to a consumer in (state) XYZ, which has a (different type of) plain language law, which law applies?

The traditional rule of law is that a contract that is valid where made is fully enforceable in another state. Under this rule the retailer from ABC would assert that its written contract with the consumer in XYZ was made in ABC and that the contract, being valid and in compliance with the laws of ABC, should be enforced by the courts of XYZ. The consumer, however, could claim that although the underlying terms and provisions of the contract might

29

be valid under the law of ABC (and even of XYZ), the format or procedure in which those terms are written is subject to the law of XYZ, where he or she lives.

If the consumer's contention is upheld by the courts of XYZ, the ABC retailer has the very difficult problem of complying with many different states' plain language laws, some of which might contradict each other. On the other hand, if the retailer's position is upheld by the courts, a business located in a state with a lax or no plain language law would have a distinct advantage over businesses in states with stringent plain language laws, and the benefits of plain language laws would be lost to certain consumers or consumer transactions.

Is there any means of avoiding such difficulties, complexities, and confusion with the plain language movement, one of whose underlying tenets is eliminating confusion and complexity? As with most things in law, no absolute answer can be given. But there are two possible directions toward a "yes" answer. The first would be for the commissioners of Uniform State Laws to prepare a uniform plain language law for adoption by all the states.

However, there are drawbacks to this solution. It would undoubtedly take several years for the commission to draft a proposed uniform law. Once the bill is drafted and presented to the states, it could take several more years for most or all states to enact it, just as it took many years for most states to enact the Uniform Commercial Code. Last, each state is free to modify the uniform proposed act, as some states did to various parts of the Uniform Commercial Code.

The second means of avoiding the problems of multiple plain language laws would be for Congress to enact a federal plain language act that would totally preempt and supersede all state and local laws and regulations on the topic. Some critics of federal action will object that such a move would leave no room for variations to meet local needs and experiments to see how the plain language concept works. Proponents of a preemptive federal plain language law may well assert, however, that the part of the consumer market that has written contracts is no longer local, but nationwide.

Although there may be some problems for business in dealing with different states' plain language laws in general, it would still seem to be in the best interest of business not to oppose the passage of such laws. The reason is that essentially it will be difficult to present a valid position for general total opposition. Also, by not opposing such laws, business interests can work with appropriate legislative committees and agencies in the process of drafting and passing plain language laws so that they contain provisions that are reasonable and under which business can function.

4

Federal Law

AS discussed in Section 3, it may generally be best for business if the plain language law becomes a universal federal law. It would also appear to be best for the consumer, so that the consumer does not become trapped between different plain language laws and will be covered when dealing with out-of-state businesses.

A federal law has been proposed in Congress. In its present form it appears to be inflexible and overly strict. It does not contain a provision allowing a business to defend itself by pleading a good faith effort at compliance. Also, in its present form it does not preempt all state laws on the subject, so it would not provide a single uniform national standard.

The proposed law is H.R. 12212 of the 95th Congress, 2nd Session, as follows:

> To amend the Truth in Lending Act to require that contracts and agreements respecting credit transactions subject to the Act be written in clear and understandable language.

"Be it enacted by the Senate and House of Representatives of the United States of America in Congress assembled, That chapter 1 of the Truth in Lending Act is amended by adding at the end thereof the following new section:

§ 116. Use of clear and understandable language

Each contract or agreement to which a consumer is a party respecting any consumer credit transaction shall be:

1. written in nontechnical language and in a clear and coherent manner using words with common and everyday meaning; and

2. appropriately divided and captioned by its various sections.

Sec. 2. The table of sections of Chapter 1 of the Truth in Lending Act is amended by inserting at the end thereof the following new item:

116. Use of clear and understandable language.''

As with state legislative action in this area, it would appear to be prudent for business interests not to ignore this proposed federal law or to oppose the entire underlying concept. Rather, it would appear to be in the interests of business to work for a reasonable federal plain language law, one that allows the defense of a good faith effort at compliance, that preempts all state laws, and that is not too strict and inflexible.

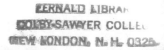

5

Possible Future Developments

BEYOND the immediate issue of passage of state and federal laws and regulations, other points and possible developments should be noted. The plain language movement does not appear to be a passing political fad. On a broad scale the plain language movement in the law could reinforce the call on all levels of the educational system of the country to upgrade English language courses. Many complaints have been voiced in recent years that even college graduates cannot read and write English competently. All levels in the American educational system may feel reinforced by the plain language movement in their desire to upgrade courses on writing. Law schools may have to consider instituting courses on plain language legal writing. Businesses may need to start in-house courses on writing and/or send certain employees to such courses. Such a trend would probably first be discernible in consumer goods and service businesses.

A sizable amount of criticism has been directed at television and other mass media for diluting the language. The advertising industry has also been a target of criticisms and complaints. For instance, it was recently reported that when primary school students were asked to spell the word "relief" some answered "ROLAIDS."

It is possible that commercial advertisements, particularly ads that promote consumer products, will be made subject to plain language laws. Although the government is not allowed to restrict freedom of the press and of speech in many types of mass communication, these prohibitions are not fully applicable to commercial advertising. For instance, the government can prohibit in advance the publication of advertisements that are fraudulent or untrue, even though it cannot do the same for publications of a political, public, or scientific nature that are untrue. Therefore, the constitutional provisions on freedom of the press and speech would probably not bar the application of plain language laws to the general field of advertising. Most consumer advertisements contain only plain words (and sometimes nonexistent words), but they do not always use them in a clear and coherent fashion, particularly when they combine them with sound (music, sound effects, and so on) and pictures.

Although a considerable portion of consumer advertising is directed at local markets and is on behalf of local merchants, much of it is for the national market. It is in its national advertising that the advertising industry could get into trouble as it tried to satisfy different state plain language laws. Consequently, it may consider supporting a preemptive federal plain language law.

The general informed opinion is that the nation's first plain language law (New York State) does not apply to insurance policies. However, other states will not necessarily follow the same path, and it is likely that the insurance industry will find itself covered by one or more states' laws. As regards their content and terms, insurance policies must comply with the law of the state in which the policyholder or insured lives at the time the policy is issued. Consequently, the insurance industry already has considerable experience in dealing with a multitude of state laws on one topic.

At present, insurance is the one major American industry over which there is very limited federal control. Therefore, if a preemptive federal plain language law inclusive of insurance policies were passed by Congress, it would constitute one of the first major broad-scale federal actions concerning this industry. It is possible that the insurance industry might lobby for its exclusion from such a federal law for this reason, but that is mainly a matter of politics.

An area of the economy that is related to, but separate from, the field of insurance is pensions. The application of plain language laws to pension plans—particularly corporate and union pension plans—would constitute another substantial application of new law to this field. In recent years pensions have been increasingly subjected to governmental control and regulation, particularly under the Federal Employees Retirement Income Security Act. The impetus behind including pension agreements and plans in plain language laws is the same as that behind other applications of such laws—so that the potential retiree can fully understand his pension.

A recent court decision, which did not involve the U.S. Employees Retirement Income Security Act, held that a long-time union member could not be denied his pension because of a brief interruption in his employment service. Under the technical "fine print" provisions in his plan this brief interruption disqualified him from receiving a pension. In part the court's judgment in this case was based on its finding that under appropriate federal law this pension was a security; nonetheless, equitable principles, which also underlie the plain language movement, appear to have played a part in the decision. This decision may add to the drive to include the pension field within the coverage of plain language laws.

The securities market and industry are fields to which plain language laws may be applied. At the first level, contracts, if in writing, between brokerage houses and their individual customers may have to be put in plain English. This will happen if the individual purchaser of securities is considered a consumer under the law. Going beyond individual contracts, it may develop that the terms, including the accounting sections, in prospectuses for stocks and bonds offered for sale to the general public will have to be written in plain language (if they are viewed as part of the contract of sale).

The terms of mortgages and various trust indentures underlying corporate bonds, if they are also considered a part of such contracts, may have to be written in plain language. A bit more remote, but still possible, is that the terms contained in publicly sold stock certificates—both common and preferred—will have to meet the same requirements. It is even possible that the very contents of corporate charters and bylaws, if construed as more than a contract between the corporation and the chartering government, will be considered part of the contract of sale of a corporation's securities and therefore subject to such laws.

Another area that may in time be affected by plain language laws is that of computers. Computers are a major and growing instrumentality in the American economy and society, and plain language laws will probably interact with the operations and effects of these machines. At present the computer field, like many other specialties, has its own "language," which is sometimes called computer talk or computer speech. The best generally known word of computer speech is "input."

As a means of communication, computer speech is often difficult for people who are not in the field. As the computer increases its entry into consumer economic areas it may become necessary to apply the plain language concept to it. If this happens it may pose a lot of problems to those in the computer field, because many of the underlying premises in computer technology and use are extremely intricate. Their "translation" into plain language could prove to be far more troublesome than rewriting the "legalese" in contracts.

A much broader potential development than those discussed immediately above would be the introduction of plain language into contracts wholly between businesses. One direction such a development could take would be a demand by small businessmen that plain language laws be passed or amended to cover their contracts with the larger business entities with which they deal. Examples of such written agreements between small and large businesses are products supply contracts, equipment leases, and franchise agreements. In such areas small businessmen might view themselves as being equal or parallel to ordinary consumers. The political weight of the small business community on state legislatures is considerable and cannot be ignored.

Another means by which plain English could become prevalent in business contracts would simply be by its steady absorption into the general contract writing process rather than by legislation. If plain language permeates consumer contracts widely in the future, it may well become a general method of drafting most contracts. Although such a development might add to the general efficiency of the business community, it does not necessarily mean that businessmen will operate without the legal establishment. The legal profession will still function as it traditionally has in the area of contracts; that is, it will deal with the wording of contracts and the effects of such wording on the operation of diverse fields of law.

The last potential development we will discuss in relation to the plain language movement might be called "what's good for the goose is good for the gander." It is the possibility that government regulations and the actual laws enacted by legislatures will have to be written in plain English. Many statutes (laws) are difficult even for attorneys to understand and they often pose problems for courts in trying to interpret and apply them. Both the general public and business might justifiably demand that lawmakers write laws in understandable terms, especially if they pass laws requiring businessmen to write contracts in plain language.

The arena of government regulations covering business is extensive. Many local, state, and federal regulations are written in highly technical terms—in so-called bureaucratese. Businessmen to whom such regulations apply often cannot understand them, and, therefore, find it difficult to comply. The result may be unintentional violations. Although it may be argued that some regulations require technical wording, sound positions can be and have been advanced that many of the intricacies of wording are neither justified nor required. If the plain language movement becomes general, business will have more support for its request that government regulations be written in generally understandable words and terms.

6

Implementation and Forms

IT is the purpose of the following discussion to provide some general ideas on how to implement changes under plain language laws. However, this discussion should not be considered either a formal or an informal legal opinion; nor can it take the place of a technical compliance manual. It should be borne in mind that each type of business has its own specific consumer contracts with their own components, and that each state has its own substantive laws, including those on various types of contracts. In rewriting contracts to comply with plain language laws businessmen should continue to rely on their usual means of drafting contracts, including heeding the advice of qualified advisors. One thing business should do is keep carefully detailed records of action taken and time and money spent to comply with plain language requirements so as to be able to document its good faith effort at compliance.

The process of revising and/or rewriting consumer contracts and forms is probably best initiated by a complete review of the contract in question. You cannot simply rewrite a contract line by line by replacing long phrases and technical words with short sentences and simpler words. A contract is and must be dealt with as an entity; it is not just a collection of separate provisions, sections, and paragraphs. Frequently the different parts of a contract are interrelated and interact on one another.

When rewriting a contract in plain language, business should strongly consider conferences between those doing the rewriting and operations personnel to effect practical coordination of the process and to let the right hand know what the left hand is doing.

In the initial review of the contract before rewriting begins, an analysis of the underlying concepts contained in the wording should be made. Sometimes an underlying concept is no longer operative. For example, certain time credit purchase contracts and loan agreements contain wage assignment provisions. Such a means of collecting a defaulted debt has been prohibited by law in some states. If that has happened in your state, the entire wage assignment provision can be eliminated.

Other times a concept underlying a provision in the existing contract may no longer be considered reasonable or practical. There may have been changes in court or other legal procedures through the years, adverse public reaction to the enforcement of a provision's concept, other forms of outmodedness, or changes in the long-range advertising and public relations objectives and plans of a business. Again, in such instances, the entire provision can be dropped.

Some concepts may be very difficult, if not impossible, to translate into plain English. For instance, the concept underlying the Rule of 78's provisions on prepayment interest rebates in loan agreements is difficult to set out plainly. It may in some cases be replaced with a flat prepayment fee, say $25, and/or a direct pro-rata interest rebate, depending on local state laws. (As a side note, there has been some movement in certain legislative bodies to prohibit the Rule of 78's.)

If a business changes a concept because the old one is difficult to write in simple form, it may even find an advertising opportunity to promote itself, its new concept, and its products. Thus the initial step in contract rewriting is a thorough review of the existing agreement, with the opportunity to reject, revise, or modify underlying concepts and to create new ones.

In the actual rewriting of the provisions of a contract it will generally be found that the new (plain language) agreement is considerably longer than its technical or "legalese" predecessor. This will be true unless a great many old concepts and their written embodiment in provisions have been deleted during the review process. Many of the terms of the old agreement were probably written in short but technical legal phrases, which could only be written in simplified language at greater length.

In the course of rewriting it may be found that certain "legalese" words and phrases must be retained. Many writers who have already rewritten contracts agree that if such words or phrases must be kept, plain language definitions or examples should be included. For instances, many real estate agreements contain the word "fixture," which some experts feel should be retained. Plain language requirements can be met if an example of a real property fixture, such as an oil burner, is given.

Lengthier plain language contracts will not necessarily be less complex than their predecessors. As a rule, the longer a contract is, the more complex it is, because the parts interact and may even clash with one another (unless an appropriate exception is included).

In some instances provisions in an existing contract may be part of the case or statute law of a state, and may not have to be included in the new contract. For example, an ordinary check (negotiable instrument) is simple and plain on its face. Generally its operation as a contract is also simple and direct. However, through the years a great deal of case law and statute law has built up as part of the Uniform Commercial Code, covering situations in which the contract of the check does not operate simply and smoothly. This built-up law is part of the check contract, but is not printed on the check itself. Indeed, it is so large a body of law that if it were printed on the instrument, it would make the check several pages long.

Thus it may not be necessary to set out in the new contract a concept that may have been spelled out in the old agreement but is covered by law. The new contract can simply refer to the specific law. However, opinion in the legal profession is split over whether this is enough. At a minimum no provision in a contract should be deleted or replaced by a brief reference to a law if that provision would constitute a surprise to a reasonable consumer.

In the rewriting of a contract certain technical terms can be retained without elaboration because the public knows what they mean. For example, most people understand "C.O.D." or "Cash on Delivery." The buyer is to pay for the merchandise when it is delivered to him. His failure to pay not only bars his receipt of the merchandise, it may also constitute a breach of the contract on his part. It does not constitute a breach of contract by the seller for refusing to deliver the merchandise. Probably none of these details has to be spelled out in a contract that contains the term "C.O.D."

In the rewriting process, when a word or phrase that has a common everyday meaning is used, that meaning should not be modified or changed by adding a new definition in writing. To do so would contradict the purposes of plain language laws. Also, any difficulty, confusion, or loss resulting from such a change would probably be held against the business that made the change. Under the legal rule of construction of contracts the courts are likely to decide that any ambiguity in a contract is to be held against the party that wrote it or submitted it to the other party.

According to some people who have already rewritten contracts into plain language, a degree of simplification can be achieved by replacing Greek- or Latin-derived words with words that have a Germanic or Middle English base. Words with Germanic or Middle English roots are part of the common everyday language of the average person in English-speaking countries.

Historically, the common people of England spoke a Germanic-based language when they were conquered by the Normans, who spoke an earlier form of Latin-based French. The conquering Normans became the upper class, and the lower class essentially retained its Germanic tongue. In succeeding centuries people who received a formal education in England, including the members of the legal profession, were trained in Greek and Latin. In part to distinguish themselves from the illiterate common populace, in part because Greek and, more particularly, Latin had become a major part of their written vocabulary, and in part because Latin frequently had (single) words for concepts English did not, members of the legal profession incorporated words derived from the two classical languages into the law.

In more recent times the use of classically based and Latin words in the law has been largely an attempt to exhibit educational attainments, because through the centuries English has developed a wide and comprehensive vocabulary of its own. The older, Germanic-based part of the language has continued to contain the more common words.

Included here for informational purposes only are a few sample forms of plainly worded contracts (Exhibits 3 to 5). Before using such forms it should be ascertained that they comply with all laws affecting the locale in which they are going to be used and that no copyright laws are being violated.

Exhibit 3. Partial example of simplified lease agreement.

T 186—Apartment lease, 2-5 family dwelling,   PREPARED BY ARNOLD MANDELL, L.L.B.   © 1978 BY JULIUS BLUMBERG, INC.,
plain English format, 11-78   PUBLISHER, NYC 10013

LEASE AGREEMENT

The Landlord and Tenant agree to lease the Apartment at the Rent and for the Term stated on these terms:

LANDLORD:..   **TENANT:**..

Address for Notices:..   ....

                                                        ....

Apartment (and terrace, if any) ....at................

Lease date:	Term	Yearly Rent $ ....
...........19.......	beginning..........19.......	Monthly Rent $ ....
	ending..........19.......	Security $ ....

Rider   Additional terms on.............page(s) initialed at the end by the parties is attached and made a part of this Lease.

1. Use

The Apartment must be used only as a private Apartment to live in and for no other reason. Only a party signing this Lease and the spouse and children of that party may use the Apartment.

2. Failure to give possession

Landlord shall not be liable for failure to give Tenant possession of the Apartment on the beginning date of the Term. Rent shall be payable as of the beginning of the Term unless Landlord is unable to give possession. Rent shall then be payable as of the date possession is available. Landlord will notify Tenant as to the date possession is available. The ending date of the Term will not change.

3. Rent, added rent

to pay the added rent on time, Landlord shall have the same rights against Tenant as if Tenant failed to pay rent. Payment of rent in installments is for Tenant's convenience only. If Tenant defaults, Landlord may give notice to Tenant that Tenant may no longer pay rent in installments. The entire rent for the remaining part of the Term will then be due and payable.

4. Security

Tenant has given Security to Landlord in the amount stated above. If Tenant fully complies with all of the terms of this Lease, Landlord will return the Security after the Term ends. If Tenant does not fully comply with the terms of this Lease, Landlord may use the Security to pay amounts owed by Tenant, including damages. If Landlord sells or leases the Building, Landlord may give the Security to the buyer or lessee. Tenant will look only to the buyer or lessee for the return of the Security.

5. Services

Landlord will supply: (a) heat as required by law, and (b) hot and cold water for bathroom and kitchen sink. Stopping or reducing of service(s) will not be reason for Tenant to stop paying rent, to make a money claim or to claim eviction. Damage to the equipment or appliances supplied by Landlord, caused by Tenant's act or neglect, may be repaired by Landlord at Tenant's expense. The repair cost will be added rent.

Tenant must pay for all electric, gas, telephone and other utility services used in the Apartment and arrange for them with the public utility company.

Landlord may stop service of the plumbing, heating, elevator, air cooling or electrical systems, because of accident, emergency, repairs, or changes until the work is complete. If unable to supply any service because of labor trouble, Government order, lack of fuel supply or other cause not controlled by Landlord, Landlord is excused from supplying that service. Service shall resume when Landlord is able to supply it.

6. Repairs

Tenant must take good care of the Apartment and all equipment and fixtures in it. Tenant must, at Tenant's cost, make all repairs and replacements whenever the need results from Tenant's act or neglect. If Tenant fails to make a needed repair or replacement, Landlord may do it. Landlord's expense will be added rent.

7. Alterations

Tenant must obtain Landlord's prior written consent to install any panelling, flooring, "built in" decorations, partitions, railings or make alterations or to paint or wallpaper the apartment. Tenant must not change the plumbing, ventilating, air conditioning, electric or heating systems. If consent is given, the alterations and installations shall become the property of Landlord when completed and paid for, and shall remain with and as part of the Apartment at the end of the Term. Landlord has the right to demand that Tenant remove the alterations and installations before the end of the Term. The demand shall be by notice, given at least 15 days before the end of the Term. Landlord is not required to do or pay for any work unless stated in this Lease.

Exhibit 4. Plain language special trust plan form.

SUMMARY OF AGREEMENT:

THE TRUST IS FOR THE BENEFIT OF THE SETTLOR FOR LIFE AND THEREAFTER THE PRINCIPAL IS DISTRIB- UTED TO HIS ESTATE.

THIS AGREEMENT, delivered in New York City on   , 19   , between the Settlor,   , of   , and the Trustee, CITIBANK, N.A., of New York City,

WITNESSETH:

The Settlor transfers to the Trustee cash in the amount of   Dollars ($), and such other property, if any, described in Schedule A, to be held, with any additions, IN TRUST, to invest and reinvest the same and to dispose of income and principal as follows:

FIRST—DISPOSITION OF INCOME AND PRINCIPAL

During the Settlor's lifetime, the Trustee shall apply the net income from the Trust to the Settlor's use not more frequently than quarterly and may apply to his use so much or all of the principal of the Trust as the Trustee in its discretion may deem advisable for any purpose whatsoever. Upon the Settlor's death, the Trustee shall dis- tribute the Trust principal to the estate of the Settlor.

SECOND—TRUSTEE'S DISCRETION TO TERMINATE THE TRUST

The Trustee may at any time in its discretion terminate this Trust if in its sole judgment the Trust is so small as to make it inadvisable to continue, and it shall pay out the principal to the Settlor or, if the Trus- tee shall determine in its sole judgment that the Settlor is incapable of managing his own affairs, to the committee, conservator or other person having the care and control of the Settlor.

THIRD—TRUSTEE POWERS

In addition to those powers conferred by law, the Trustee shall have, with respect to any property at any time held by it hereunder, the power to invest and reinvest in property of any character, including participations in any one or more of the common trust funds maintained by the Trustee.

In exercising its discretion under Articles First and Second, it shall not be necessary for the Trustee to inquire as to any other income or property of the Settlor. Any decision by the Trustee, made in good faith, shall fully protect the Trustee and shall be binding and conclusive upon all persons interested in this Trust.

In connection with its investment decisions with respect to the trust fund, the Trustee shall have no duty (1) to ascertain whether any director, officer or employee of Citibank, N.A. or Citicorp (or any of their subsidiaries) possesses any information which has not been publicly disclosed and which, if generally known, might have a significant market impact or (2) to take into account any such information in making a determination as to the acquisition, retention or disposition of any investment.

FOURTH—COMPENSATION

The Trustee shall receive compensation as provided by separate agreement attached hereto, which agreement may be amended by the Settlor and Trustee.

FIFTH—RESIGNATION AND REMOVAL

Any Trustee may resign at any time by a written instrument delivered to the Settlor. The Settlor shall have the right to remove any Trustee hereunder by a written instrument delivered to the Trustee. In the event that any Trustee shall resign or be removed, the Settlor shall have the power to appoint any corporation or individual other than himself to act as successor Trustee hereunder by a written instrument delivered to the person appointed as successor Trustee. No successor Trustee shall be personally liable for any act or omission of any predecessor Trustee. Any successor Trustee shall accept without review the accounts rendered and the property delivered by or for a predecessor Trustee without incurring any liability or responsibility.

SIXTH—SETTLOR'S POWER TO CHANGE TRUST

The Settlor at any time during his lifetime by a written instrument delivered to the Trustee may amend or revoke this agreement, provided that the duties and liabilities of the Trustee shall not be changed nor its compensation decreased except with its written consent and the Settlor may withdraw amounts of principal annually from the Trust only in the amount of $1,000 or multiples thereof. The Settlor may not amend or revoke this agreement by his Will. The Settlor reserves the right for himself or any other person to increase this Trust by delivering cash or other property to the Trustee, by having the proceeds of insurance policies made payable to the Trustee or by bequest by Will all of which shall be acceptable to the Trustee.

SEVENTH—EFFECTIVE DATE AND GOVERNING LAW

This agreement shall be effective upon execution by both the Settlor and the Trustee. It shall be governed and construed in all respects according to the laws of the State of New York.

(Continued on p. 48)

                                        _____
                                               Settlor

                                        CITIBANK, N.A., Trustee

Attest: By_____

_____
Trust Officer

STATE OF   )
                                  : ss:
COUNTY OF   )

    On this   day of   , 19   , before
me personally came   , to me known and
known to me to be the individual described in and who executed the
foregoing instrument, and he acknowledged to me that he executed the
same.

                              _____
                                    Notary Public

STATE OF NEW YORK   )
                       : ss:
COUNTY OF NEW YORK)

    On this   day of   , 19   , before
me personally came   , who being by me duly
sworn said that he resides in   ,
that he is a   of Citibank, N.A., the
national banking association described in and which executed the foregoing instrument; that he knows the seal of the said association; that
the seal affixed to said instrument is said association's seal and was so
affixed by authority of the Board of Directors of said association and
that he signed his name thereto by like authority.

                              _____
                                    Notary Public

Exhibit 5. Contemporary trust form—short and simple.

Plain English Trust

How This Trust Works

I set up this trust with you as the trustee. It will benefit me for my lifetime. On my death, you will pay the principal to:

_____

and the trust will end. If

_____

does not survive me, then you will pay to:

_____

Setting Up the Trust

I give you $_____ to invest for the trust.

Payments During My Lifetime

During my lifetime, you will pay me the net income of the trust. "Net income" is the income earned less your compensation. I'll receive net income payments quarterly.

I can withdraw any part or all of this trust by notifying you in writing. Each withdrawal must be for at least $1,000. Withdrawals may not be made more often than once each month.

You may use all or part of the principal in any way you believe will benefit me. Any decision you make in good faith will fully protect you and will bind everyone with an interest in this trust.

Your Investment Powers As Trustee

You may invest the funds from this trust in any assets you deem appropriate including any of the Collective Investment funds which you maintain.

I am aware that you are not allowed to use investment information known to Citibank but not generally available to the public. So, you won't be responsible for not using such information even though it might affect the value of certain investments.

Your Compensation

Your only compensation for acting as trustee will be 1% of the total value of the principal of the trust charged annually with a minimum of $250 for each full year or any part of a full year.

Adding To The Trust

I may increase the principal of this trust by delivering cash to you.

Ending The Trust

I may end this trust and withdraw all of its assets by writing to you.

Changing My Beneficiaries

I may change my beneficiaries by writing to you.

Payments to Incapable Persons

You needn't pay principal or net income to anyone who in your judgment is incapable of managing his own affairs. Instead, you may pay the person having care or control of the incapable person, whether court appointed or not, or you may use it in any other way you believe will benefit the incapable person. You will add to principal any income payment you don't make.

Payments To Persons Under The Age of 21

You needn't pay the principal or net income to any person under the age of 21. Instead, you may pay in any way you believe will benefit such person. You will add to the principal any income payment you don't make. When such person reaches the age of 21, you will pay him his remaining principal. If he dies before, you will pay his estate.

Resigning

You may resign as trustee anytime by notifying me in writing or the person then having care and control of any incapable person.

No Other Changes

I cannot make any other changes in this trust by my Will or otherwise.

Law That Governs

This trust will be governed by New York State law.

Date Of This Agreement

This agreement will begin on the date you and I both sign it. I may, however, cancel it by writing to you within 10 days of this agreement. If I do, I won't incur any charges or fees, except for out-of-pocket expenses you may have had before my written cancellation reaches you.

_____

Your Name

_____

Trustee

7

Glossary

TO show how language can be simplified, we are listing many technical (legalese) words frequently used in existing contracts, with their definitions in simpler words or phrases. You should be aware that, as with the discussion on implementation in Section 6, you cannot simply lift this glossary without thought and hope to rewrite a contract in plain English. Business should continue to use its usual means of drafting contracts, including relying on qualified advisors' opinions, to prepare its plain language contracts. In cases of possible confusion in the glossary the abbreviations (n) for noun and (v) for verb are used to identify those parts of speech.

accelerate	cause to happen immediately, quickly, now, or sooner
acceptor	one who receives or accepts a bill of exchange or other instrument
accommodation (financial)	adjustment or settlement

accrue (v)	increase, add to, come into being, become due
addendum	addition and/or change
adjudicate	have a court make a decision or decide a dispute
adjudication	court decision on a dispute
administrator	appointed official who handles property
advance (of money or credit)	to give or grant funds
advance (v)	to move up
alteration	change
annum	a year
appropriate (v)	to take or obtain possession
ippropriation (n)	a taking, takeover
sessment	money due, usually as a tax on property
ignee	one who receives (an assignment or transfer)
gnment	a transfer
assignor	one who gives or makes an assignment or transfer
sume (v)	to take on or add to
a fide	real, true, and actual
attel mortgage	lien on personal property
collaterize	to put up collateral or security
comment (v)	to start or to begin
commencement	start or beginning
commingle	to mix different things or property together
comprise	to make up, create, or constitute; to consist of
compromise (n)	an agreement reached by each party giving up part of its claim(s), right(s), or property
compromise (v)	to give up part of a claim, right, or property to reach an agreement
conclusive	final and absolute
concurrent	to occur at the same time
concurrently	at the same time
conservator	a person or official appointed to gather, handle, and protect property
consideration	value, generally in the form of money, goods, services, promises, and so on
construe	to explain, determine, decide, or decipher
contingency	a condition
contingent	dependent on
co-signer	one of two or more signers
countermand	to revoke or reverse an order, decision, or direction
covenant (v)	to promise or agree
covenantor	one who makes a promise or covenant

curtail	to end, reduce, or cut back
debit	a deduction or subtraction, usually from an account
deficiency	a shortage, usually in an account, contract, or project-job
demised	designated; usually used in phrases such as "demised premises" instead of the real subject, such as a leased house
discharge	to release, usually from an obligation
dishonor	to refuse to pay, accept, receive, or honor
disposition	a disposal, getting rid of, or sale
effectuate	to carry out or to carry into effect
empower	to give power or authority to
endorse	to sign
endorsee	one who receives an instrument signed on the back by another
endorsement	a signature
executor	usually a court-appointed person designated to handle an estate or other property
executory contract	a contract for something to be done or to take effect in the future
fixture	a piece of personal property that is so attached to a real property as to become a permanent part of it, such as an oil burner
forbear	to withhold taking action or exercising a right
forbearance	the act of forbearing
grant	to give, transfer, or allow
grantee	one who receives something from someone else
grantor	one who gives or grants something to someone else
guarantee or guaranty (n)/(v)	a promise, pledge, or agreement to back up the living up to the terms of an agreement or contract by someone else
guarantor	one who agreees to back up the living up to the terms of an agreement by someone else
hereafter	after or later
hereinafter	further along, later on, or afterward
heretofore	before or prior
honor	to pay, accept, or receive
inadvertence	a mistake, oversight, or accident
incur	to take on or accept
indebted	to be in debt
indebtedness	the state of being in debt or having a debt

indenture	a document, contract, deed, lease, mortgage, or similar instrument, usually dealing with real property—instead of using the word "indenture," it would be simpler to name the actual document; for example, lease
indorse, indorsee, indorsement	variations of endorse, endorsee, endorsement
induce	to urge on or to lead into
insofar (as)	as far (as)
instrument	usually a document, such as a contract
intangible personal property	personal property that cannot be touched physically such as a contract right or an ownership interest in a corporation
irrevocable	not capable of being ended, revoked, altered, or terminated
joint tenants	two or more people with equal rights and obligations in an agreement, land, or other holding that cannot be amended in any way without the consent of all
jointly	(as in jointly and severally) together, along with, or together with
laches	wrongful or unwarranted delay, holding back, or failure
liquidate	to end something, such as a business, including disposing of its assets
liquidation	the ending of something, such as a business, including the disposal of its assets
mature	to be due and, therefore, owing or payable
matured	the state of being due and, therefore, owing
merge	to combine two or more things together into one or to absorb
merger	the combining of two or more things together into one, or the absorption, as of one or more corporations by another
misfeasance	performance of a legal act in an illegal manner
misrepresentation	an untruth or lie
modification	a change
modify	to change
mortgagee	a person who receives a mortage on property, usually as security for a loan—it might be simpler to designate a mortgagee as the "lender" or "seller" in contracts or other documents

mortgagor	a person who gives a mortgage (security instrument) on property he owns, usually as security for a loan—it might be simpler to designate a mortgagor as the "borrower" or "buyer" in contracts or other documents
negotiable	capable of being freely transferred without restriction or change, such as a check
negotiable instrument	a document such as a draft or check
nonnegotiable	incapable of being transferred at all or transferable only under limited conditions and not freely, such as a contract to perform work
obligation	debt or duty
obligee	a person to whom a debt or duty is owed—it would be simpler to call an obligee a "creditor," "lender," or "seller"
obligor	a person who owes a debt or duty—could be called a "debtor" or "buyer"
payee	a person who receives or is to receive money as payment
payer or payor	a person who pays or is obligated to pay
per annum	yearly or annually
per centum	percent
per diem	per day, by the day, or daily
perform	to do, act, carry out
personal property	all property that is not land, buildings, or fixtures
pledge (n)	a promise
pledge (v)	to promise
pledgee	a person who receives or is the beneficiary of a promise—usually can be called a "lender" or "seller"
pledger or pledgor	a person who makes a promise; basically, a debtor, buyer, or borrower
principal	the body of an amount due or loaned
proceedings (legal) (n)	a lawsuit
promisee	a person who receives or is the beneficiary of a promise—usually a lender or seller
promisor or promiser	a person who gives a promise—usually a borrower, debtor, or buyer
punctual	on time, performed at the time due
purchaser	buyer
quantum	amount or quantity